PHONICS **BOOK 5**

Double Letter Vowels

YBM

Contents

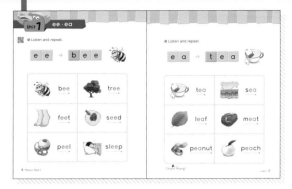

Letters and Sounds
Combinations of letters and the target sounds are introduced.

Words
Students learn to recognize the words that have the beginning, middle, or ending sounds of the target letters.

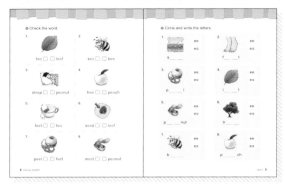

Practice
Students practice choosing the correct word or letters for the given pictures.

Check and Write
Students practice checking and writing the correct double letters for the target words.

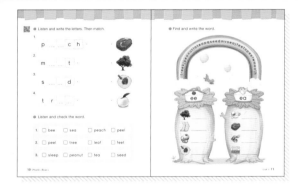

Listen and Check
Students further practice identifying the sounds and the words by reading and listening.

Write
Students review the double letter vowels and words of the unit.

Let's Read
Students practice the target sounds and words by reading simple sentences.

Choose and Write
Students practice reading the sentence and choosing the correct word.

◦ Review & Challenge ◦

The Review provides practice of the materials from the previous four units by using a variety of exercises focusing on the target sounds of letters and words.

The Challenge offers sessions to review the entire book. It reinforces students' phonics skills with various exercises and a test.

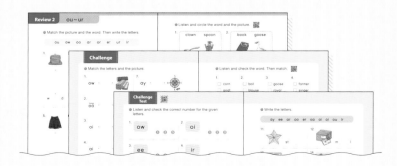

Special Features

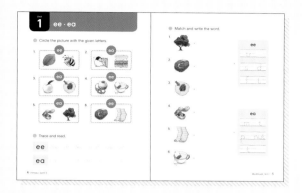

✿ Workbook ✿

Students review what they learned in class.
This can be used as homework or further practice.

✿ How to use QR codes ✿

Scan QR codes on the content pages, then you can use all of the listening sounds and flash animations, such as chants, stories, and listening questions.

e-learning

Scan e-learning QR codes, then you can use e-learning for self-study.

game

Scan game QR codes, then you can enjoy the phonics games.

• Note for Teachers •

The ultimate goal of the book is to help students be able to read and write words even if they encounter a new word. Therefore, students should be encouraged to listen and to identify the sounds of the letters, not to memorize the spellings of the words.

Unit 7 — ee · ea

 Listen and repeat.

e e → b e e

bee	tree
feet	seed
peel	sleep

● Listen and repeat.

tea

sea

leaf

meat

peanut

peach

Chant Along!

● Check the word.

1. 
tea ☐ ☐ leaf

2. 
sea ☐ ☐ bee

3. 
sleep ☐ ☐ peanut

4. 
tree ☐ ☐ peach

5. 
feet ☐ ☐ tea

6. 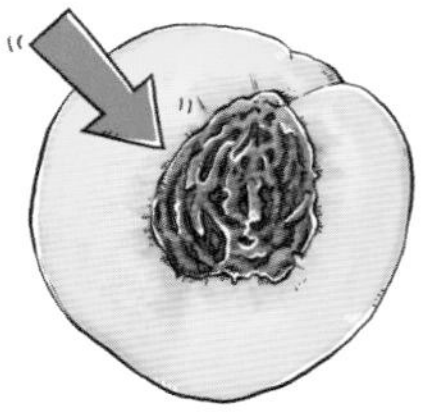
seed ☐ ☐ leaf

7. 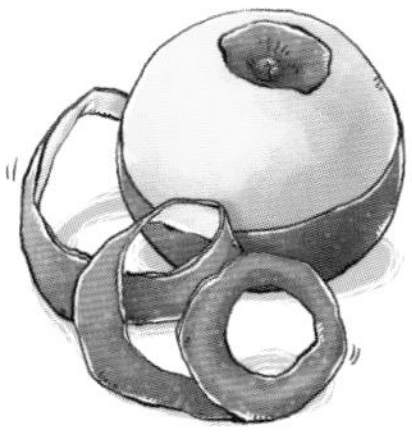
peel ☐ ☐ feet

8. 
meat ☐ ☐ peanut

● Circle and write the letters.

1.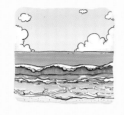

   ee

   ea

   s ___ ___

2.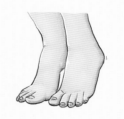

   ee

   ea

   f ___ ___ t

3.

   ee

   ea

   p ___ ___ l

4.

   ee

   ea

   l ___ ___ f

5.

   ee

   ea

   p ___ ___ nut

6.

   ee

   ea

   tr ___ ___

7.

   ee

   ea

   b ___ ___

8.

   ee

   ea

   p ___ ___ ch

● Listen and write the letters. Then match.

1.

p ___ ___ c h ·

2.

m ___ ___ t ·

3.

s ___ ___ d ·

4.

t r ___ ___ ·

● Listen and check the word.

1. ☐ bee   ☐ sea   ☐ peach   ☐ peel

2. ☐ peel   ☐ tree   ☐ leaf   ☐ feet

3. ☐ sleep   ☐ peanut   ☐ tea   ☐ seed

Find and write the word.

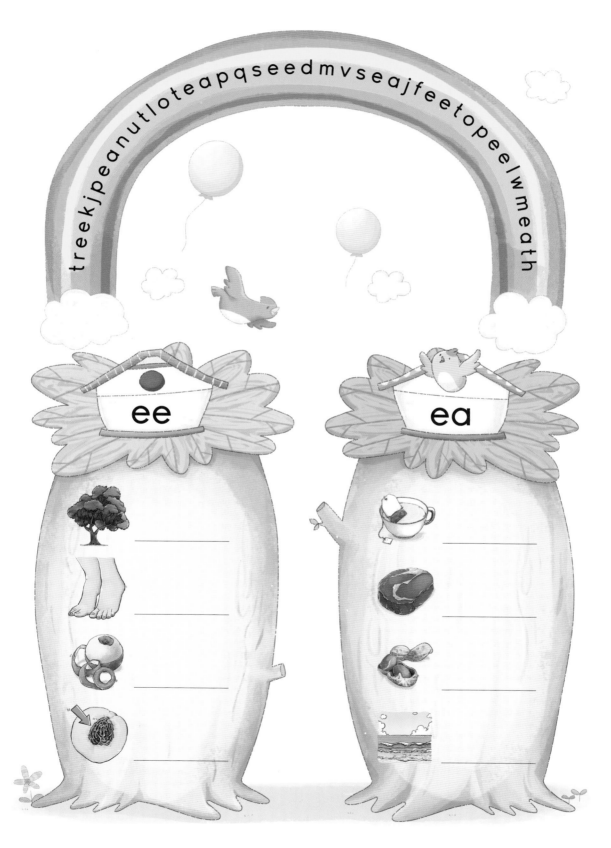

ee

ea

A boy bee sleeps on the leaf.

A girl bee comes to the tree.

"Wake up, wake up! Time to eat!"

The boy bee on the leaf gets up.

"Okay! I'll make tea for you."

The girl bee says,

"Then I'll peel a peanut and a peach for you."

● Circle and write the correct word.

1. There is a _____ on the leaf.

   seed   meat

2. A bee drinks a cup of _____.

   leaf   tea

3. The girl eats a _____ under the tree.

   peel   peach

4. A bee has shoes on six _____.

   feet   tree

5. The boy is cooking _____.

   meat   leaf

🔘 Listen and repeat.

a i → r a i n

rain ------▶	train ------▶
mail ------▶	nail ------▶
rail ------▶	tail ------▶

● Listen and repeat.

gray

tray

clay

play

hay

May

● Check the word.

1.

clay ☐ ☐ mail

2.

play ☐ ☐ train

3.

tray ☐ ☐ May

4.

gray ☐ ☐ nail

5.

clay ☐ ☐ train

6.

tail ☐ ☐ rail

7.

May ☐ ☐ rain

8.

mail ☐ ☐ hay

Circle and write the letters.

1.

ai
ay

gr __ __

2.

ai
ay

r __ __ l

3.

ai
ay

tr __ __ n

4.

ai
ay

M __ __

5.

ai
ay

pl __ __

6.

ai
ay

n __ __ l

7.

ai
ay

tr __ __

8.

ai
ay

t __ __ l

● Listen and write the letters. Then match.

1.

m ___ ___ l ·

·

2.

t r ___ ___ ·

·

3.

r ___ ___ n ·

·

4.

p l ___ ___ ·

·

● Listen and check the word.

1. ☐ hay   ☐ play   ☐ train   ☐ tail

2. ☐ May   ☐ nail   ☐ clay   ☐ mail

3. ☐ tray   ☐ rail   ☐ gray   ☐ rain

● Find and write the word.

tail   clay   mail

nail   tray

hay   rain   May

ai

ay

My family is on the train.

The train runs fast on the rail.

The rain is falling.

I play with the clay inside.

What do I make?

I make grapes and bananas on a gray tray.

They look good!

● Circle and write the correct word.

1. The children play on the _____.

   May   hay

2. The _____ is on the tray.

   mail   rain

3. The girl has a toy _____.

   train   gray

4. A dog with a short _____ is on the mat.

   nail   tail

5. The boy makes a car with _____.

   clay   tray

Unit 3   oa · ow

🔊 Listen and repeat.

o a → b o a t

boat

coat

soap

road

goat

toast

● Listen and repeat.

o w → b o w l

bowl - - - - - - - →

row - - - - - - - →

snow - - - - - - - →

pillow - - - - - - - →

window - - - - - - - →

yellow - - - - - - - →

Chant Along!

Circle the word.

1.

row   toast

2.

coat   road

3.

pillow   goat

4.

boat   bowl

5.

soap   snow

6.

yellow   road

7.

window   boat

8.

bowl   toast

Write the letters.

oa   ow

1.

s ___ ___ p

2.

b ___ ___ t

3.
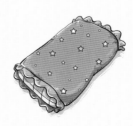
pill ___ ___

4.

yell ___ ___

5.

t ___ ___ st

6.

r ___ ___

7.

r ___ ___ d

8.

b ___ ___ l

9.

sn ___ ___

🔵 Listen and circle the picture.

1.

2.

3.

4.

5.

6.

🔵 Listen and write the word.

| yellow | row | bowl | soap | pillow | road |

1. _____

2. _____

3. _____

4. _____

● Find and write the word.

boat

bowl

window

snow

road

row

soap

goat

oa

ow

Lonely Goat gets up early in the morning.

He washes his face with soap.

Then he eats toast on a plate
and soup in a bowl.

Oh, the world is covered in snow.

He puts on a yellow coat and a red scarf.

Now he is ready to go to school.

● Choose and write the word.

| boat | window | goat | row | coat |

1.
The girl cleans the _____s.

2.
The _____ is covered in snow.

3.
The boy puts on a yellow _____.

4.
The girl _____s the boat.

5.
A _____ eats grass.

 e-learning   game

🔵 Listen and repeat.

o i → c o i n

coin

point

oil

boil

soil

foil

● Listen and repeat.

boy

toy

joy

oyster

soybean

royal

Chant Along!

Circle the word.

1.

boy   soil

2.

foil   joy

3.

oil   oyster

4.

boil   royal

5.

toy   coin

6.

oyster   point

7.

soybean   oil

8.

joy   boil

Write the letters.

oi   oy

1.
j _____ _____

2.
s _____ _____ l

3.
p _____ _____ nt

4.
b _____ _____ l

5.
t _____ _____

6.
r _____ _____ al

7.
_____ _____ ster

8.
c _____ _____ n

9.
f _____ _____ l

Listen and circle the picture.

1.

2.

3.

4.

5.

6.

Listen and write the word.

foil   point   joy   oyster   royal   oil

1. _____

2. _____

3. _____

4. _____

● Find and write the word.

coin

soil

royal

oyster

toy

point

foil

joy

oi

oy

Roy and Joy are cooks.

They make dishes for a royal party.

Roy puts some soybeans and water in a pot.

He boils it on the stove.

Joy wraps some oysters and oil in foil.

She cooks them on the grill.

They are great cooks.

● Choose and write the word.

coin　oyster　toy　royal　boy

1. They are the _____ family.

2. The cook wraps an _____ in foil.

3. The boy puts a _____ in a pot.

4. It is a big _____ box.

5. The _____ wants to be a great cook.

 e-learning　 game

⬤ Circle the letters and write the word.

1.

oy   ow

_____

2.

ea   oa

_____

3.

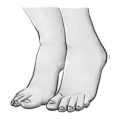

ay   ee

_____

4.

oi   ai

_____

5.

oa   ea

_____

6.

ow   ea

_____

7.

ay   ee

_____

8.

oy   oi

_____

9.

oy   ai

_____

Listen and circle the picture.

1.

2.

3.

4.

5.

6.

Listen and circle the word.

1. oyster   goat   2. seed   hay

3. meat   coin   4. train   sea

5. peel   May   6. soap   snow

Listen and write the letters. Then circle the correct picture.

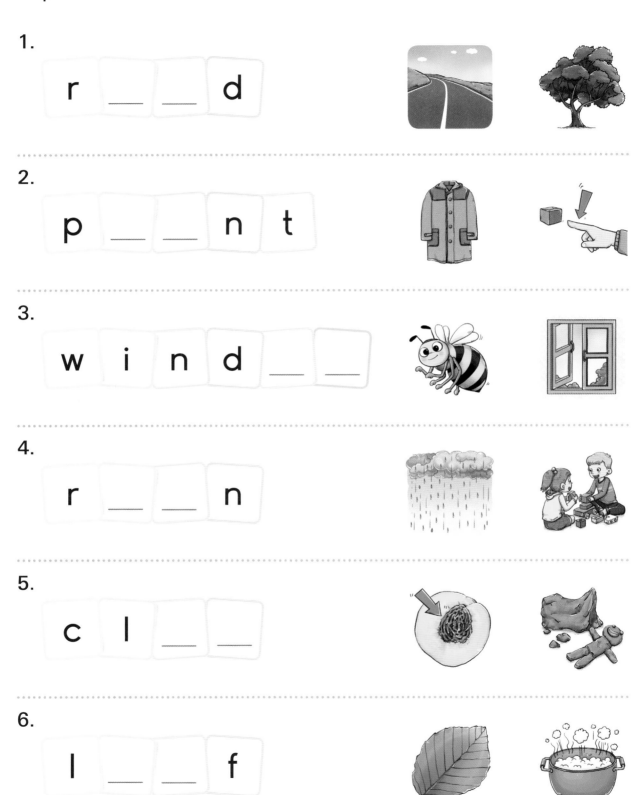

Write the word.

1.

_____

- - - - - - - - - - -

_____

2.

_____

- - - - - - - - - - -

_____

3.

_____

- - - - - - - - - - -

_____

4.

_____

- - - - - - - - - - -

_____

5.

_____

- - - - - - - - - - -

_____

6.

_____

- - - - - - - - - - -

_____

7.

_____

- - - - - - - - - - -

_____

8.

_____

- - - - - - - - - - -

_____

9.

_____

- - - - - - - - - - -

_____

10.

_____

- - - - - - - - - - -

_____

11.

_____

- - - - - - - - - - -

_____

12.

_____

- - - - - - - - - - -

_____

 Listen and repeat.

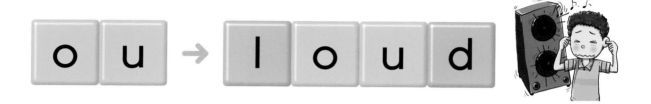

o u → l o u d

loud

cloud

ground

blouse

mouse

south

Listen and repeat.

cow

owl

brown

gown

clown

crown

Circle the letters.

1.

ou
ow

2.

ou
ow

3.

ou
ow

4.

ou
ow

5.

ou
ow

6.

ou
ow

7.

ou
ow

8.

ou
ow

● Circle and write the word.

e c o w u b r o w n f c l o u d m o

1.

_____

- - - - - - - - - - - - - -

_____

2.

_____

- - - - - - - - - - - - - -

_____

3.

_____

- - - - - - - - - - - - - -

_____

l o u d k j m m o u s e c l o w n p

4.

_____

- - - - - - - - - - - - - -

_____

5.

_____

- - - - - - - - - - - - - -

_____

6.

_____

- - - - - - - - - - - - - -

_____

s g o w n h r o w l b w p s o u t h

7.

_____

- - - - - - - - - - - - - -

_____

8.

_____

- - - - - - - - - - - - - -

_____

9.

_____

- - - - - - - - - - - - - -

_____

● Listen and circle the picture. Then write the word.

1.

_____

_____

2.

_____

_____

3.

_____

_____

4.

_____

_____

● Listen and check the word.

1. ☐ loud   ☐ ground   ☐ crown   ☐ mouse

2. ☐ cow   ☐ blouse   ☐ south   ☐ clown

3. ☐ ground   ☐ brown   ☐ owl   ☐ cloud

● Find and write the word for the picture.

owl   ground   south

crown   blouse   brown

cow   cloud

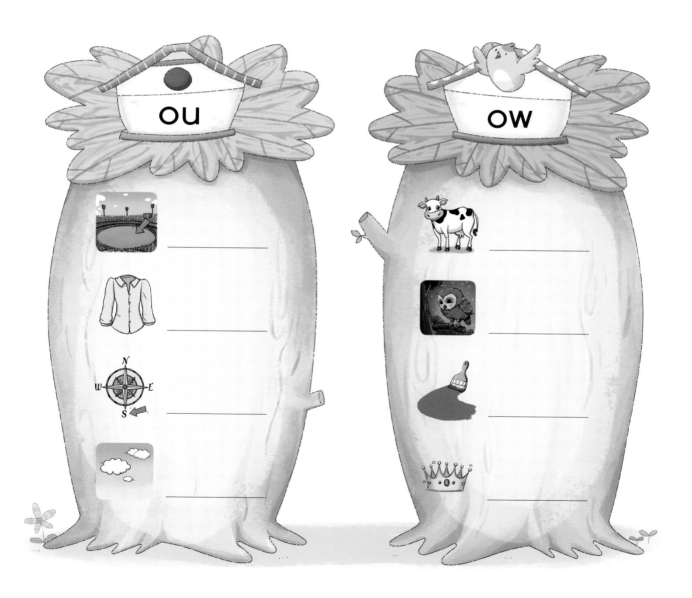

The girl goes to her grandma's house.

She smells the sweet flowers.

She sings songs in a loud voice.

Oh, she is lost.

A little brown mouse helps her.

"Look, there is grandma's house."

"Thank you, mouse!"

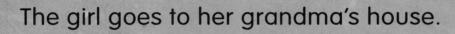

South

Unscramble and write the word.

1.
A _____ smells the flowers.

o   w   c

2.
There is a crown on the _____.

n   o   u   g   r   d

3.
A _____ with a crown goes to the south.

l   o   w   c   n

4.
The girl wears a _____ and pants.

o   u   b   s   l   e

5.
An _____ sleeps on a tree.

o   l   w

Unit 6 oo

● Listen and repeat.

o o → m o o n

moon

spoon

food

pool

root

goose

Listen and repeat.

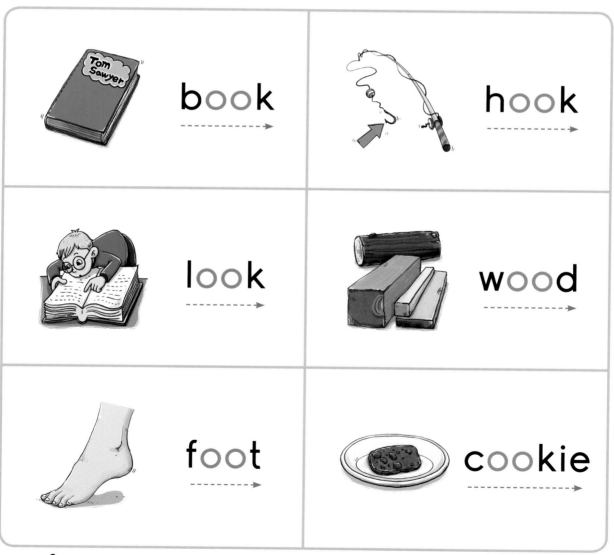

book

hook

look

wood

foot

cookie

Chant Along!

Circle the picture with the same vowel sound as the given word.

1. look

2. pool

3. foot

4. moon

5. cookie

6. root

● Circle and write the word.

r s r o o t p w o o d k y p o o l j

1.

_____

2.

_____

3.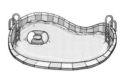

_____

l m o o n o t h h o o k c b o o k y

4.

_____

5.

_____

6.

_____

l o o k n s p o o n e c f o o t v g

7.

_____

8.

_____

9.

_____

A Listen and circle the picture. Then write the word.

1. _____

2. _____

3. _____

4. _____

B Listen and check the word.

1. ☐ wood ☐ root ☐ moon ☐ hook

2. ☐ spoon ☐ cookie ☐ food ☐ pool

3. ☐ foot ☐ look ☐ goose ☐ book

● Find and write the word for the picture.

spoon   wood   root

cookie   look

pool   hook   food

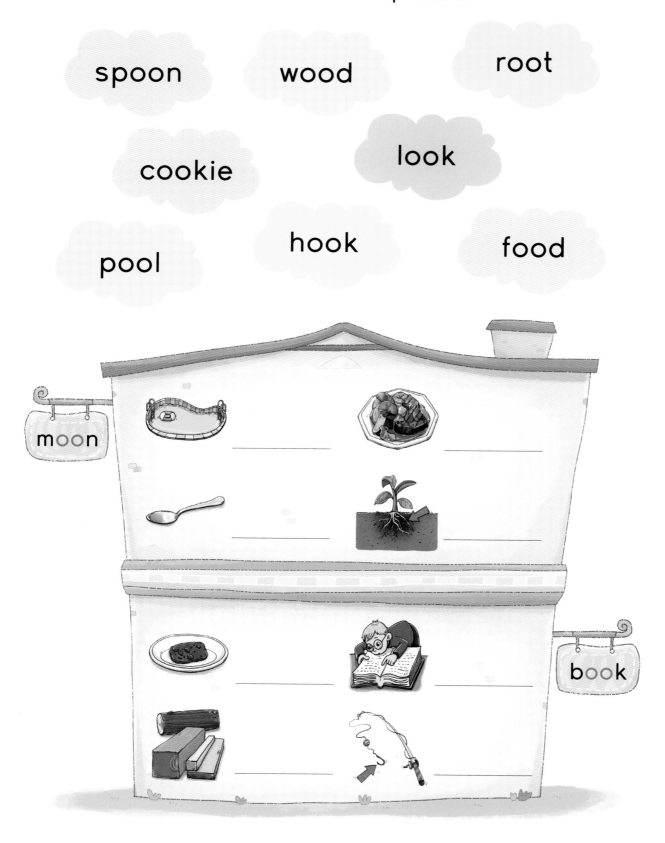

moon

book

It is a summer day.

I sit on the wood.

I read a book and eat some cookies.

Suddenly, a goose comes down and swims in the pool.

It comes to me and quacks.

I give it a cookie.

It beats its wings. It looks happy.

Unscramble and write the word.

1.

The girl is eating soup with a _____.

n o o p s

2.

The boy swims in the _____.

o p o l

3.

A goose looks at the _____.

o o m n

4.

The boy gives the girl some _____.

o o d f

5.

This is a _____.

h k o o

 e-learning game

Unit 7 ar · or

● Listen and repeat.

a r → s t a r

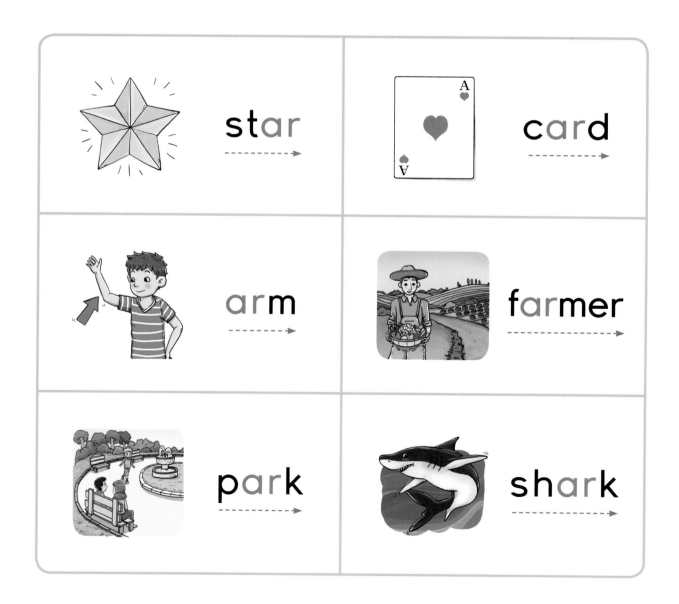

star

card

arm

farmer

park

shark

Listen and repeat.

fork

corn

horn

horse

north

store

Circle the letters.

1.

ar
or

2.

ar
or

3.

ar
or

4.

ar
or

5.

ar
or

6.

ar
or

7.

ar
or

8.

ar
or

● Write the letters.

ar   or

1.

| s | t | | |

2.

| c | | | d |

3.

| h | | | s | e |

4.

| f | | | k |

5.

| | | | m |

6.

| n | | | t | h |

7.

| f | | | m | e | r |

8.

| s | t | | | e |

9.

| h | | | n |

🔘 Listen and circle the picture.

1.

2.

3.

4.

5.

6.

🔘 Listen and circle the letters. Then write the word.

1.
ar　　or

_____

- - - - - - - - - - - -

_____

2.
ar　　or

_____

- - - - - - - - - - - -

_____

3.
ar　　or

_____

- - - - - - - - - - - -

_____

4.
ar　　or

_____

- - - - - - - - - - - -

_____

● Find and write the word for the picture.

star

north

arm

horse

card

shark

fork

corn

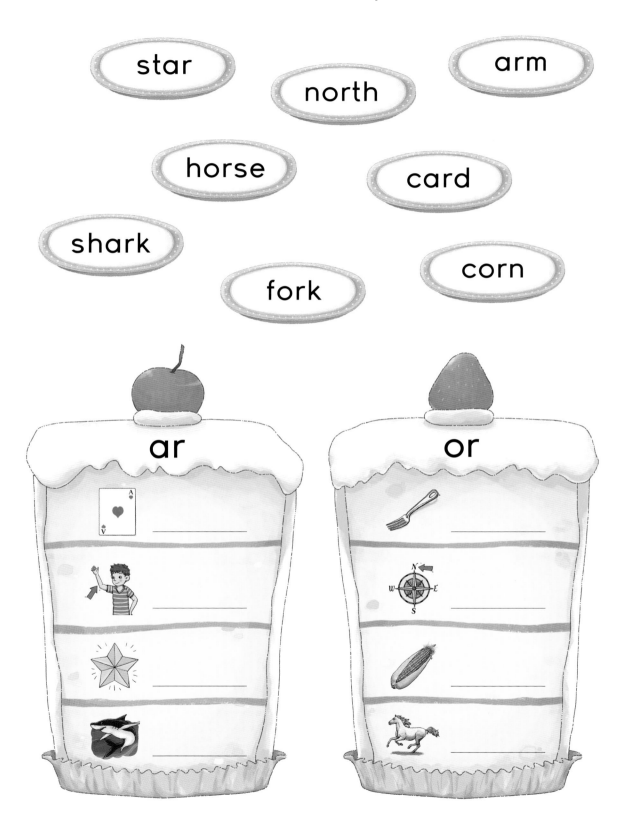

ar

_____

_____

_____

_____

or

_____

_____

_____

_____

My dad and mom are farmers.

They grow corn on their farm.

They raise horses, too.

They start working before the sun comes up.

They finish working after the stars come up.

They are very busy.

● Choose and write the correct word.

> card　　farmer　　park　　shark　　store

1.

   The _____s are Tom's parents.

2.

   A _____ is a fish.

3.

   The children play _____s.

4.

   The man works at the ice-cream _____.

5.

   The horse is in the _____.

● Listen and repeat.

i r → g i r l

g**ir**l	b**ir**d
b**ir**thday	sk**ir**t
sh**ir**t	c**ir**cle

Listen and repeat.

er → letter

ur → purse

er

letter

soccer

singer

ur

purse

purple

turtle

Chant Along!

Circle the letters.

1. 　er　ur

2. 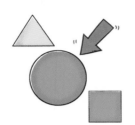　ir　er

3. 　ur　ir

4. 　ir　er

5. 　ur　er

6. 　er　ur

7. 　ir　er

8. 　ur　ir

Write the letters.

ir   er   ur

1.

| s | o | c | c | | |

2.

| s | k | | | t |

3.

| p | | | p | l | e |

4.

| g | | | l |

5.

| t | | t | l | e |

6.

| l | e | t | t | | |

7.

| s | i | n | g | |

8.

| p | | | s | e |

9.

| s | h | | | t |

🔵 Listen and circle the picture.

1.

2.

3.

4.

5.

6.

🔵 Listen and circle the letters. Then write the word.

1.
ir   er

2.
er   ur

3.
ur   ir

4.
er   ur

● Find and write the word for the picture.

bird

letter

purse

purple

skirt

circle

birthday

soccer

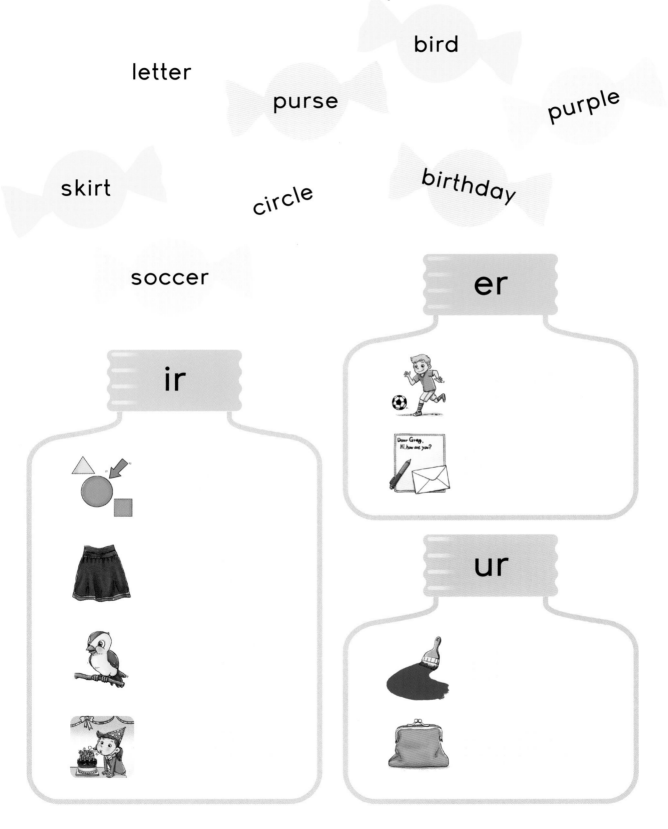

er

ir

ur

Mom and I went shopping today.

Mom bought a skirt for me.

Mom bought soccer shoes for my brother.

Mom bought a shirt for Dad.

And Mom bought a purple purse for herself.

Everybody is happy with today's shopping.

● Choose and write the correct word.

soccer   bird   letter   turtle   birthday

1.

The boy bought a small _____ .

2.

The girl is happy with a blue _____ .

3.

It is a _____ cake for Jiho.

4.

It is a fan _____ for the singer.

5.

The boy plays _____ .

Match the picture and the word. Then write the letters.

ou   ow   oo   ar   or   er   ur   ir

1.

2.

3.

4.

w ☐ ☐ d   p ☐ ☐ se   c ☐ ☐   st ☐ ☐

5.

6.

7.

8.

c ☐ ☐ n   sk ☐ ☐ t   l ☐ ☐ d   socc ☐ ☐

Listen and circle the word and the picture.

1. clown   spoon

2. book   goose

3. fork   bird

4. cloud   root

5. purple   brown

6. arm   loud

7. gown   farmer

8. letter   book

Listen and write the letters. Then match.

1.

p __ __ l ·

2.

n __ __ t h ·

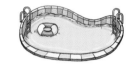

3.

g r __ __ n d ·

4.

p __ __ k ·

5.

c r __ __ n ·

6.

s k __ __ t ·

● Write the word.

1.

_____

2.

_____

3.

_____

4.

_____

5.

_____

6.

_____

7.

_____

8.

_____

9.

_____

10.

_____

11.

_____

12.

_____

Challenge

● Match the letters and the picture.

1. **ow** · ·

7. **ay** · ·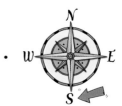

2. long **oo** · ·

8. **ou** · ·

3. **oi** · ·

9. **ee** · ·

4. **ai** · ·

10. **er** · ·

5. **ea** · ·

11. short **oo** · ·

6. **oa** · ·

12. **oy** · ·

🔊 Listen and check the word. Then match.

1.
- ☐ corn
- ☐ goat

2.
- ☐ boil
- ☐ blouse

3.
- ☐ goose
- ☐ royal

4.
- ☐ farmer
- ☐ singer

5.
- ☐ sea
- ☐ bee

6.
- ☐ train
- ☐ peel

7.
- ☐ soccer
- ☐ shark

8.
- ☐ arm
- ☐ bird

Circle and write the correct letters.

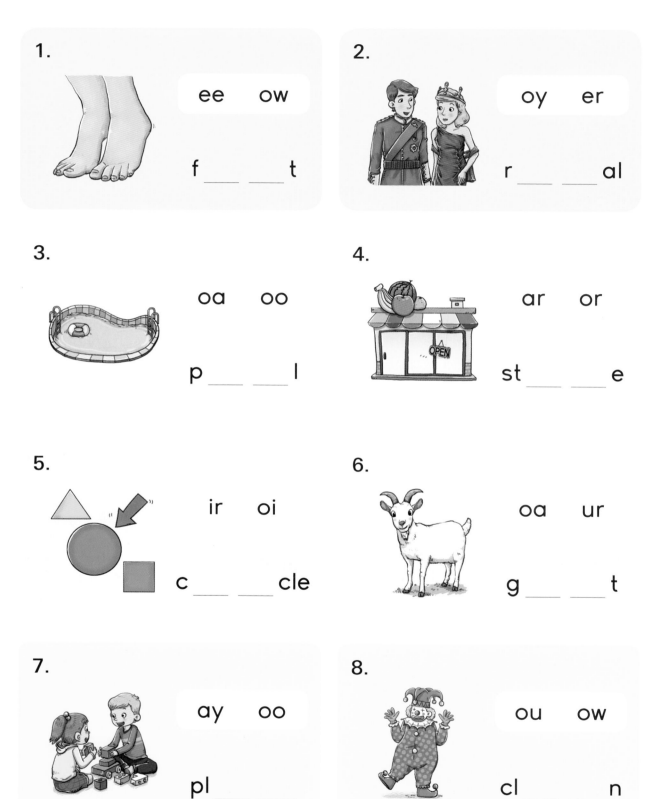

1.

ee   ow

f ___ ___ t

2.

oy   er

r ___ ___ al

3.

oa   oo

p ___ ___ l

4.

ar   or

st ___ ___ e

5.

ir   oi

c ___ ___ cle

6.

oa   ur

g ___ ___ t

7.

ay   oo

pl ___ ___

8.

ou   ow

cl ___ ___ n

Match the picture and the sentence.

1.  .

    The boy plays
with the clay.

2.  .

    The goat eats
toast and soup.

3.  .

    A bee makes tea.

4.  .

    A goose swims
in the pool.

5.  .

    Mom bought
a purple purse.

6.  .

    The cook puts
some soybeans
in a pot.

Roll a die and move the number of the spaces. If you land on a picture, say the word for the picture and spell it. If the space has a sentence, follow the directions.

Say 2 words that contain ea.

Roll again.

Go back 3 spaces.

Shortcut ➡

Say 2 words that contain oi.

Wait one turn.

Go ahead 2 spaces.

FINISH

Challenge Test

● Listen and check the correct number for the given letters.

1.
ow
① ② ③

2.
oi
① ② ③

3.
ee
① ② ③

4.
ir
① ② ③

● Listen and check the correct number.

5. ① rail   ② card   ③ gray

6. ① soap   ② mouse   ③ tea

7. ① crown   ② horn   ③ girl

8. ① leaf   ② foot   ③ bowl

9. ① turtle   ② joy   ③ loud

10. ① brown   ② wood   ③ singer

Write the letters.

ay　ee　ar　oo　er　oa　ai　oi　ou　ir

11.
st □ □

12.

m □ □ l

13.
gr □ □ nd

14.
s □ □ l

15.
socc □ □

16.

l □ □ k

17.
p □ □ l

18.

M □ □

19.

t □ □ st

20.

sh □ □ t

Period	Unit	Target Sounds	Target Words
1 2	**Unit 1**	ee, ea	bee, tree, feet, seed, peel, sleep, tea, sea, leaf, meat, peanut, peach
3 4	**Unit 2**	ai, ay	rain, train, mail, nail, rail, tail, gray, tray, clay, play, hay, May
5 6	**Unit 3**	oa, ow	boat, coat, soap, road, goat, toast, bowl, row, snow, pillow, window, yellow
7 8	**Unit 4**	oi, oy	coin, point, oil, boil, soil, foil, boy, toy, joy, oyster, soybean, royal
9	**Review 1**	ee ~ oy	
10 11	**Unit 5**	ou, ow	loud, cloud, ground, blouse, mouse, south, cow, owl, brown, gown, clown, crown
12 13	**Unit 6**	oo(long), oo(short)	moon, spoon, food, pool, root, goose, book, hook, look, wood, foot, cookie
14 15	**Unit 7**	ar, or	star, card, arm, farmer, park, shark, fork, corn, horn, horse, north, store
16 17	**Unit 8**	ir, er, ur	girl, bird, birthday, skirt, shirt, circle, letter, soccer, singer, purse, purple, turtle
18	**Review 2**	ou ~ ur	
19 20	**Challenge**	ee ~ ur	

Answers

Student Book **Answers**

• Unit 1

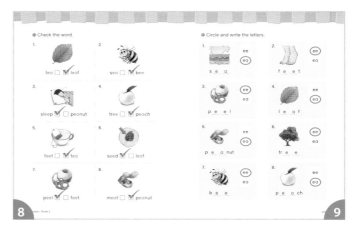

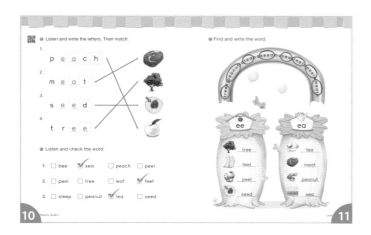

• Unit 2

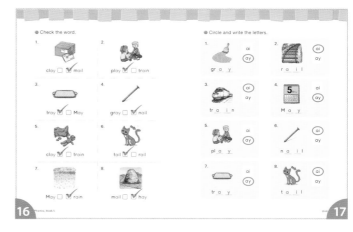

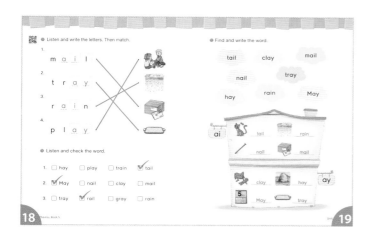

• Unit 3

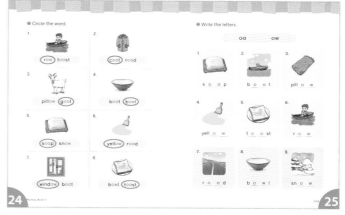

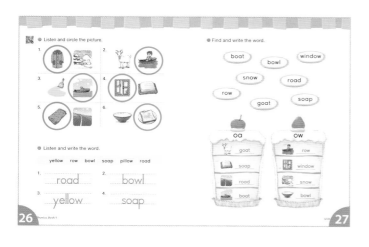

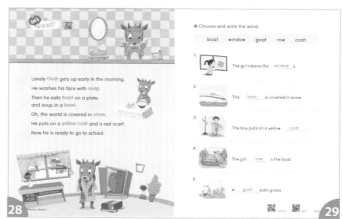

Student Book **Answers**

• Unit 4

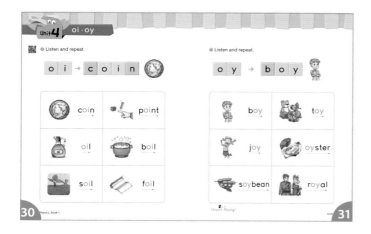

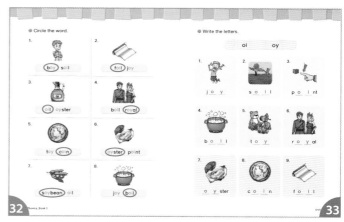

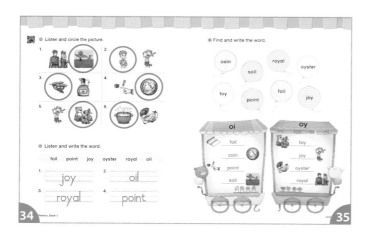

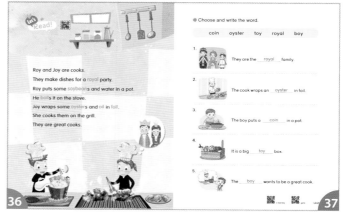

• Review 1

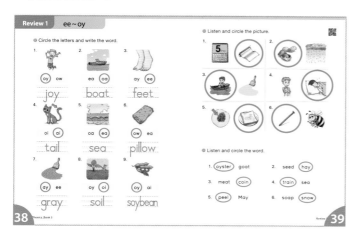

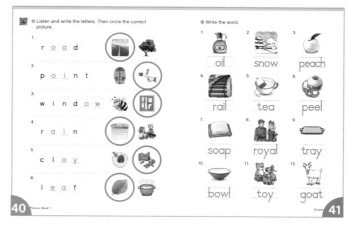

Unit 5

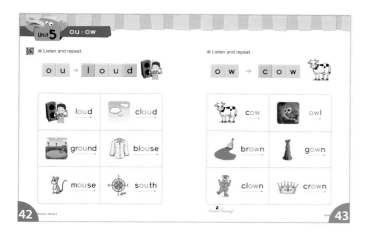

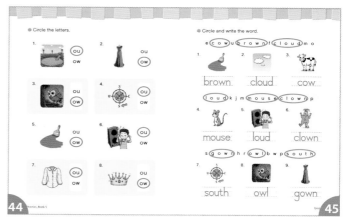

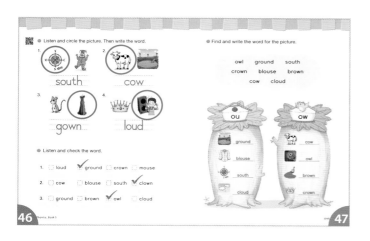

Unit 6

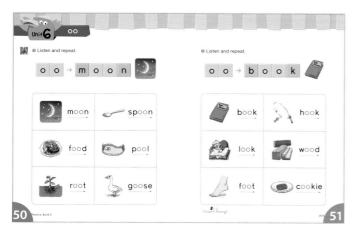

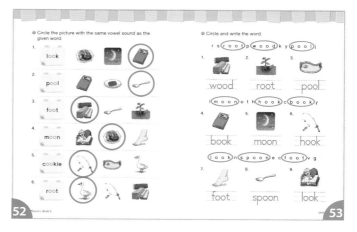

Student Book **Answers**

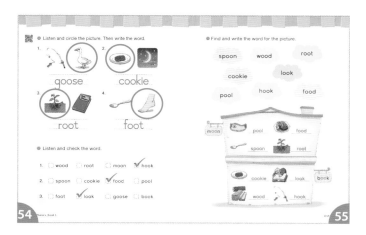

• ## Unit 7

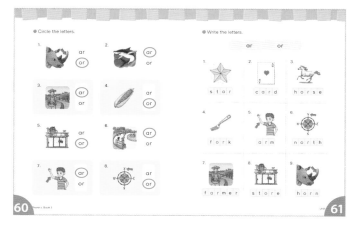

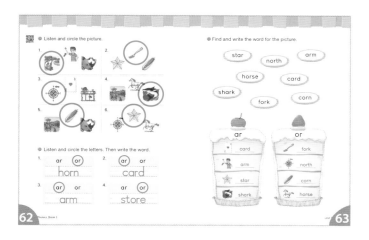

Unit 8

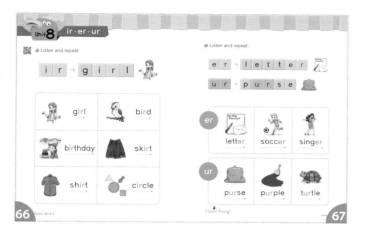

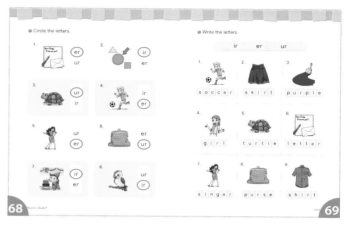

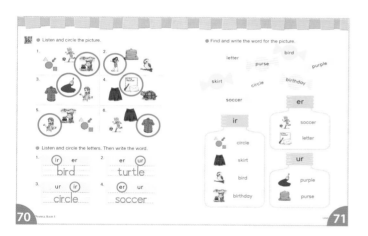

Review 2

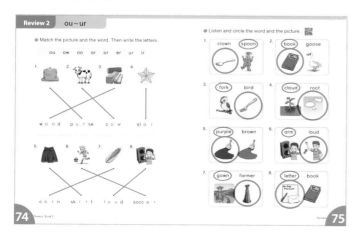

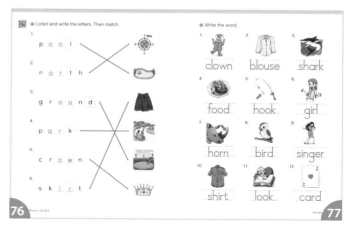

Student Book **Answers**

• Challenge

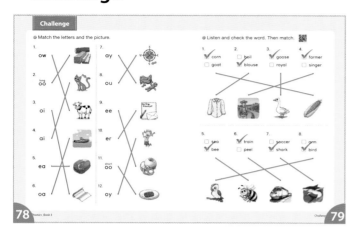

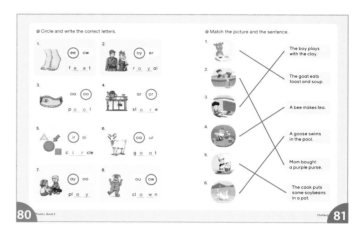

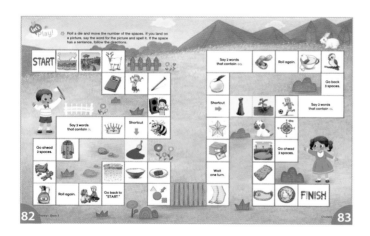

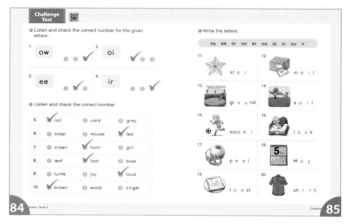

Workbook **Answers**

• Unit 1

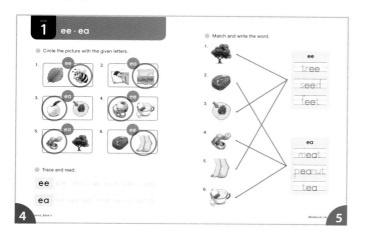

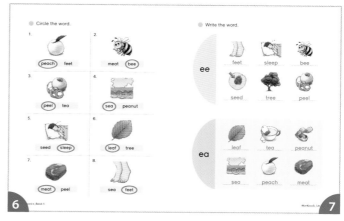

• Unit 2

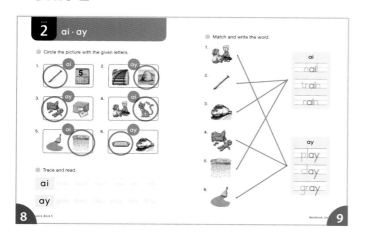

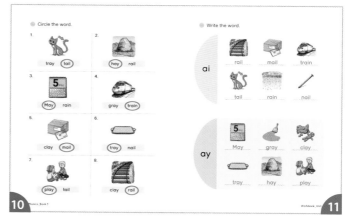

• Unit 3

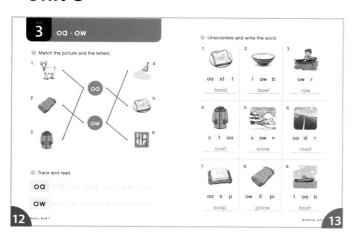

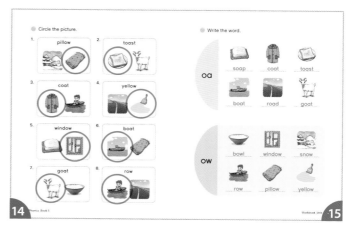

Workbook **Answers**

• Unit 4

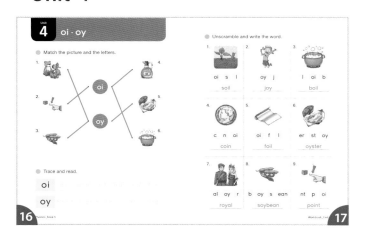

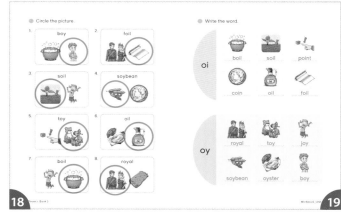

• Review 1

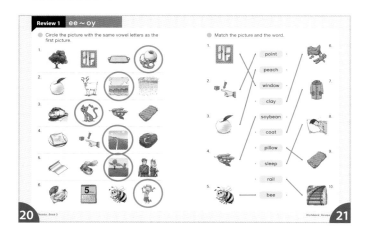

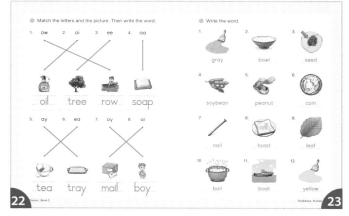

• Unit 5

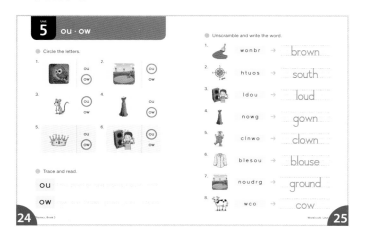

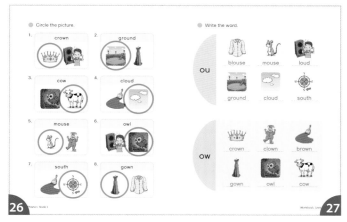

• Unit 6

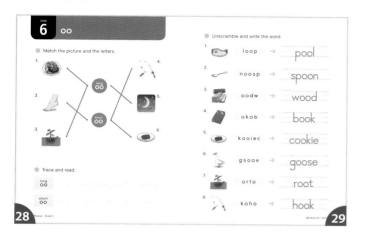

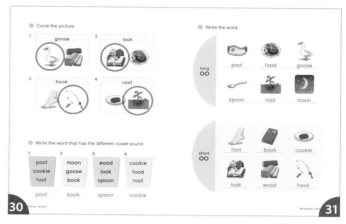

• Unit 7

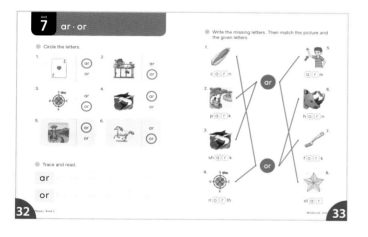

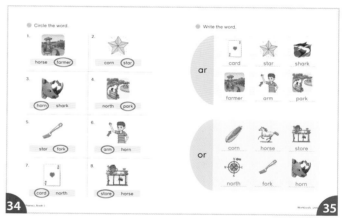

• Unit 8

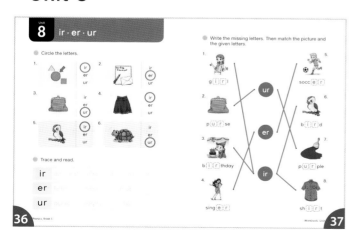

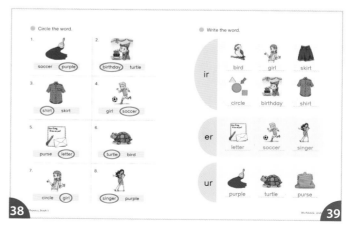

Workbook **Answers**

• Review 2

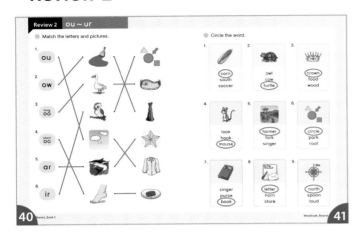

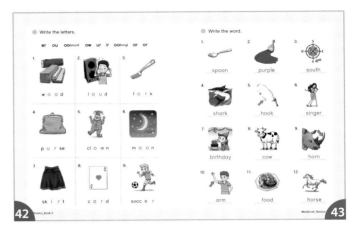

Final Test **Answers**

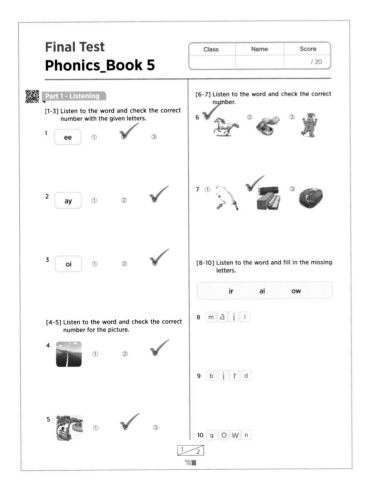

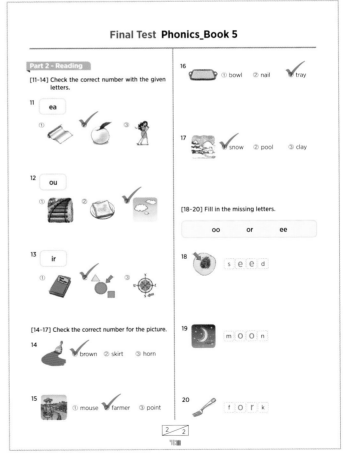

WORD CARDS

ee

ee

ee

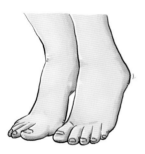

ee

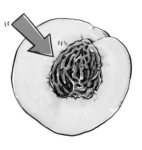

ee

ee

ea

ea

tree	bee
seed	feet
sleep	peel
sea	tea

ea

ea

ea

ea

ai

ai

ai

ai

meat	leaf
peach	peanut
train	rain
nail	mail

WORD CARDS

ai

ai

ay

ay

ay

ay

ay

ay

tail	rail
tray	gray
play	clay
May	hay

WORD CARDS

oa

oa

oa

oa

oa

oa

ow

ow

coat	boat
road	soap
toast	goat
row	bowl

WORD CARDS

ow

ow

ow

ow

oi

oi

oi

oi

WORD CARDS

pillow	snow
yellow	window
point	coin
boil	oil

oi

oi

oy

oy

oy

oy

oy

oy

foil	soil
toy	boy
oyster	joy
royal	soybean

WORD CARDS

ou

ou

ou

ou

ou

ou

ow

ow

cloud	loud
blouse	ground
south	mouse
owl	cow

OW

OW

OW

OW

long **OO**

long **OO**

long **OO**

long **OO**

gown	brown
crown	clown
spoon	moon
pool	food

WORD CARDS

long
OO

long
OO

short
OO

short
OO

short
OO

short
OO

short
OO

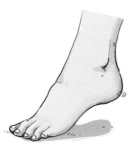

short
OO

goose	root
hook	book
wood	look
cookie	foot

WORD CARDS

ar

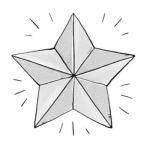

ar

ar

ar

ar

ar

or

or

card	star
farmer	arm
shark	park
corn	fork

WORD CARDS

or

or

or

or

ir

ir

ir

ir

horse	horn
store	north
bird	girl
skirt	birthday

WORD CARDS

ir

ir

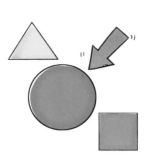

er

er

er

ur

ur

ur

circle	shirt
soccer	letter
purse	singer
turtle	purple

PHONICS LAND

Double Letter Vowels

WORKBOOK

YBM

PHONICS LAND BOOK 5

Double Letter Vowels

WORKBOOK

YBM

Contents

◎ Circle the picture with the given letters.

1. **ee**

2. **ea**

3. **ea**

4. **ee**

5. **ea**

6. **ee**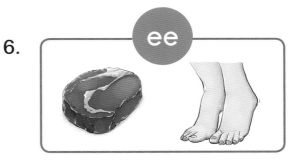

◎ Trace and read.

ee	bee tree feet seed peel sleep

ea	tea sea leaf meat peanut peach

Match and write the word.

1.  •

2.  •

3.  •

4.  •

5. 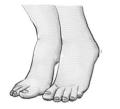 •

6.  •

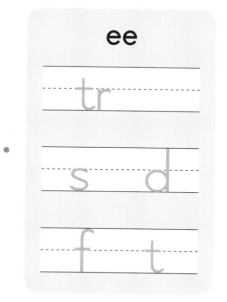

ee

tr____

s____d

f____t

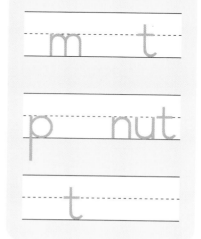

ea

m____t

p____nut

____t

Circle the word.

1.

peach   feet

2.

meat   bee

3.

peel   tea

4.

sea   peanut

5.

seed   sleep

6.

leaf   tree

7.

meat   peel

8.

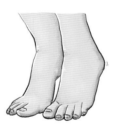

sea   feet

Write the word.

ee

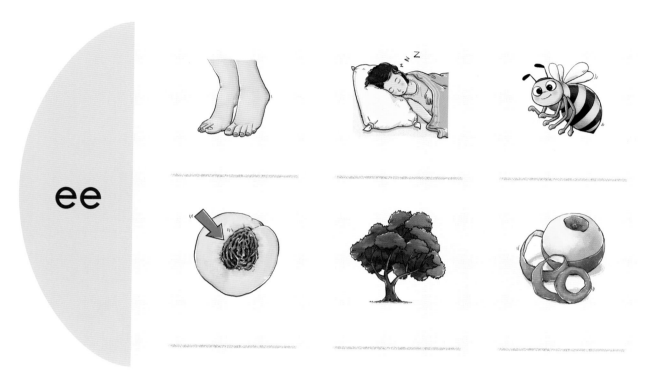

ea

Circle the picture with the given letters.

1.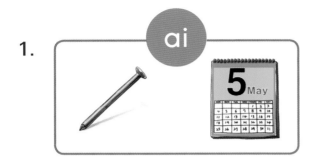

2.

3.

4.

5.

6.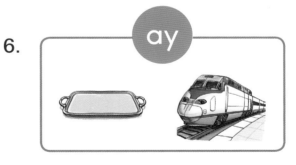

Trace and read.

ai   rain   train   mail   nail   rail   tail

ay   gray   tray   clay   play   hay   May

Match and write the word.

1.

2.

3.

4.

5.

6.

ai

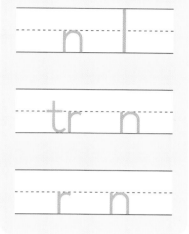

n__l

tr__n

r__n

ay

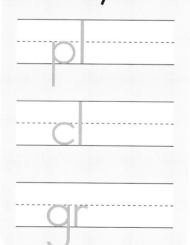

p__

cl__

gr__

Circle the word.

1.
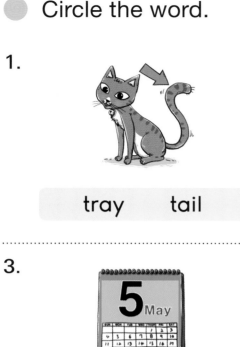
tray   tail

2.
hay   rail

3.
May   rain

4.
gray   train

5.
clay   mail

6.
tray   nail

7.
play   tail

8.
clay   rail

Write the word.

ai

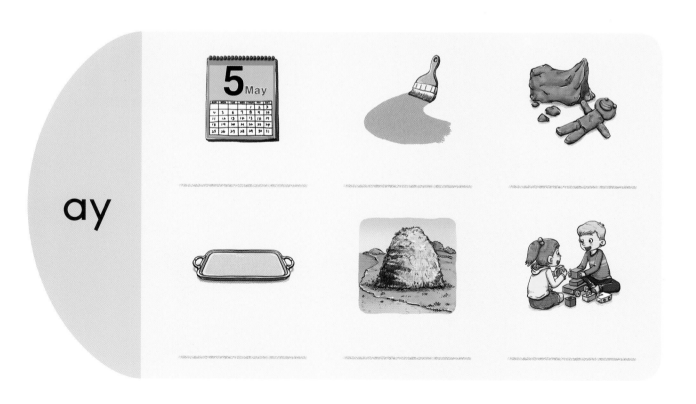

ay

Match the picture and the letters.

1.

4.

oa

2.

5.

ow

3.

6.

Trace and read.

| **oa** | boat coat soap road goat toast |

| **ow** | bowl row snow pillow window yellow |

Unscramble and write the word.

1.

oa   st   t

_____

2.

l   ow   b

_____

3.

ow   r

_____

4.

c   t   oa

_____

5.

s   ow   n

_____

6.

oa   d   r

_____

7.

oa   s   p

_____

8.

ow   ll   pi

_____

9.

t   oa   b

_____

Circle the picture.

1.
pillow

2.
toast

3.
coat
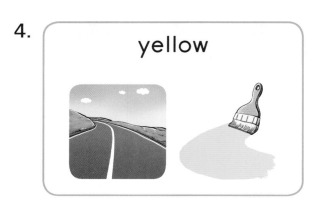

4.
yellow
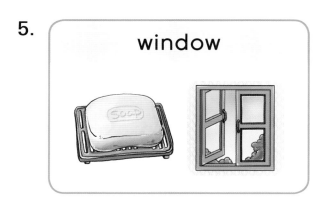

5.
window

6.
boat

7.
goat

8.
row

Write the word.

oa

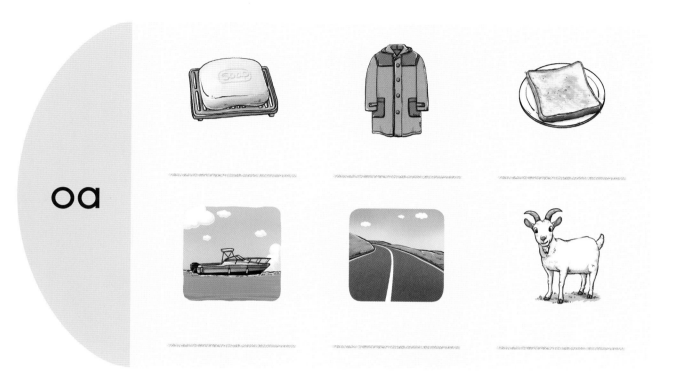

ow

⬡ Match the picture and the letters.

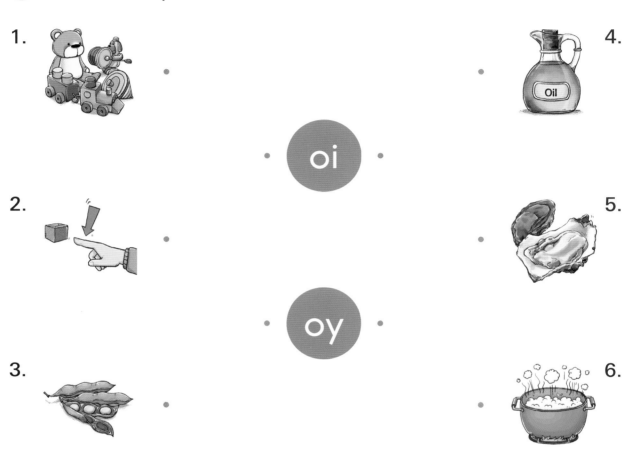

1.

2.

3.

oi

oy

4.

5.

6.

⬡ Trace and read.

oi   coin   point   oil   boil   soil   foil

oy   boy   toy   joy   oyster   soybean   royal

Unscramble and write the word.

1.

oi   s   l

_____

2.

oy   j

_____

3.

l   oi   b

_____

4.

c   n   oi

_____

5.

oi   f   l

_____

6.

er   st   oy

_____

7.

al   oy   r

_____

8.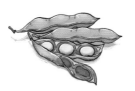

b   oy   s   ean

_____

9.

nt   p   oi

_____

Circle the picture.

1. **boy**

2. **foil**

3. **soil**

4. **soybean**

5. **toy**

6. **oil**

7. **boil**

8. **royal**

Write the word.

oi

oy

Circle the picture with the same vowel letters as the first picture.

1.

2.

3.

4.

5.

6.

Match the picture and the word.

1.

6.

• point •

• peach •

2.

• window •

7.

• clay •

3.

• soybean •

• coat •

8.

• pillow •

4.

9.

• sleep •

• rail •

5.

• bee •

10.

Match the letters and the picture. Then write the word.

1. ow   2. oi   3. ee   4. oa

_____   _____   _____   _____

5. ay   6. ea   7. oy   8. ai

_____   _____   _____   _____

Write the word.

1.

2.

3.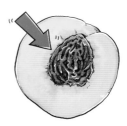

4.

5.

6.

7.

8.

9.

10.

11.

12.

◎ Circle the letters.

1.

ou

ow

2.

ou

ow

3.

ou

ow

4.

ou

ow

5.

ou

ow

6.

ou

ow

◎ Trace and read.

ou loud cloud ground blouse mouse south

ow cow owl brown gown clown crown

Unscramble and write the word.

1.  w o n b r →

2.  h t u o s →

3.  l d o u →

4.  n o w g →

5.  c l n w o →

6.  b l e s o u →

7.  n o u d r g →

8.  w c o →

Circle the picture.

1. crown

2. ground

3. cow

4. cloud

5. mouse

6. owl

7. south

8. gown

Write the word.

ou

ow

Match the picture and the letters.

1.

4.

long
oo

2.

5.

short
oo

3.

6.

Trace and read.

long oo	moon spoon food pool root goose
short oo	book hook look wool foot cook

Unscramble and write the word.

1. 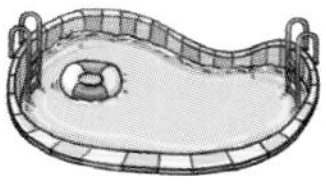 loop →

2.  noosp →

3.  oodw →

4.  okob →

5.  kooiec →

6.  gsooe →

7.  orto →

8. 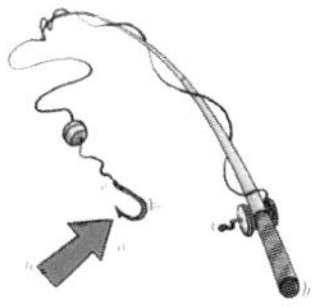 koho →

Circle the picture.

1.
goose

2.
look

3.
hook

4.
root

Write the word that has the different vowel sound.

1.

pool

cookie

foot

2.

moon

goose

book

3.

wood

look

spoon

4.

cookie

food

root

Write the word.

long OO

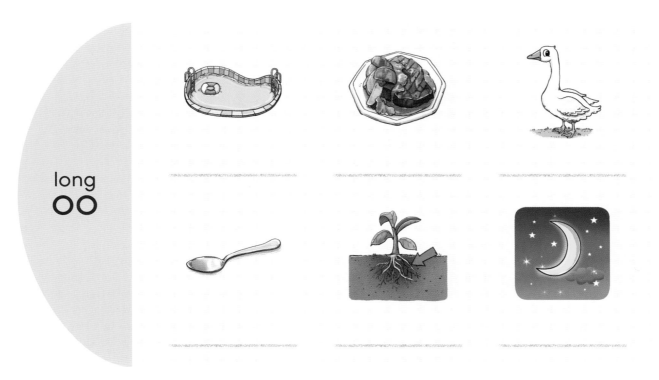

short OO

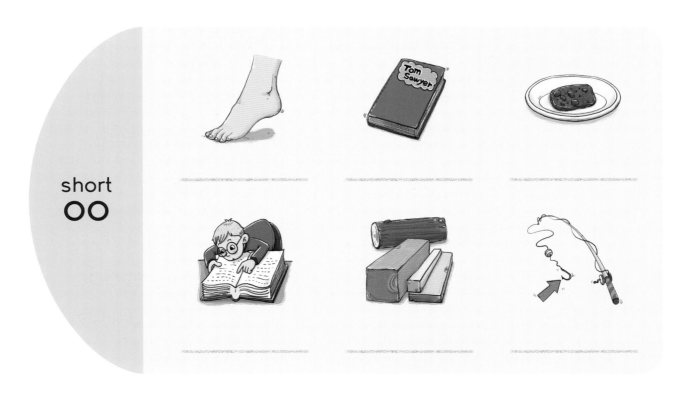

🌀 Circle the letters.

1.

ar

or

2.

ar

or

3.

ar

or

4.

ar

or

5.

ar

or

6.

ar

or

🌀 Trace and read.

ar   star card arm farmer park shark

or   fork corn horn horse north store

Write the missing letters. Then match the picture and the given letters.

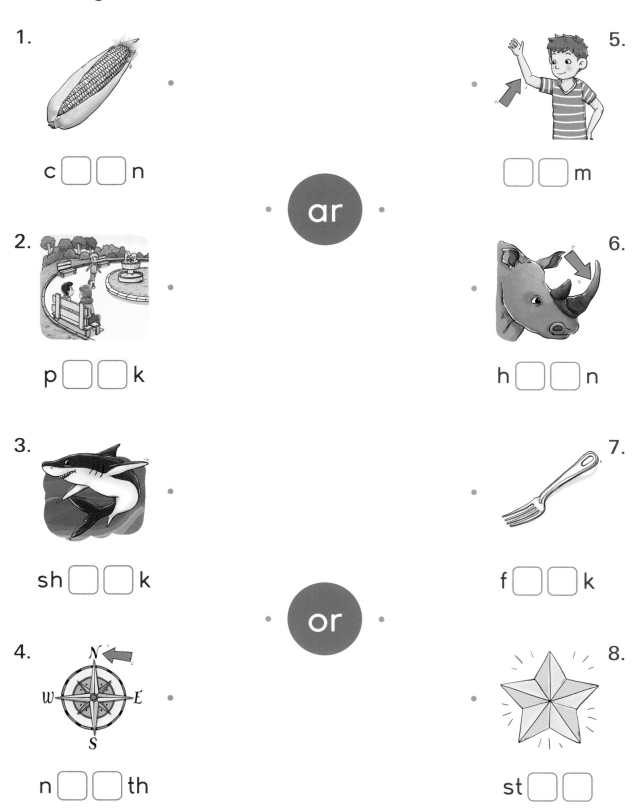

1. c ☐☐ n

2. p ☐☐ k

3. sh ☐☐ k

4. n ☐☐ th

ar

or

5. ☐☐ m

6. h ☐☐ n

7. f ☐☐ k

8. st ☐☐

Circle the word.

1.

horse   farmer

2.

corn   star

3.

horn   shark

4.

north   park

5.

star   fork

6.

arm   horn

7.

card   north

8.

store   horse

Write the word.

ar

or

Circle the letters.

1.
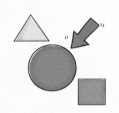
ir
er
ur

2.

ir
er
ur

3.

ir
er
ur

4.

ir
er
ur

5.

ir
er
ur

6.

ir
er
ur

Trace and read.

ir	girl bird birthday skirt shirt circle
er	letter soccer singer
ur	purse purple turtle

Write the missing letters. Then match the picture and the given letters.

1. g ⬜⬜ l

2. p ⬜⬜ se

3. b ⬜⬜ thday

4. sing ⬜⬜

ur

er

ir

5. socc ⬜⬜

6. b ⬜⬜ d

7. p ⬜⬜ ple

8. sh ⬜⬜ t

Circle the word.

1.

soccer   purple

2.

birthday   turtle

3.

shirt   skirt

4.

girl   soccer

5.

purse   letter

6.

turtle   bird

7.

circle   girl

8.

singer   purple

Write the word.

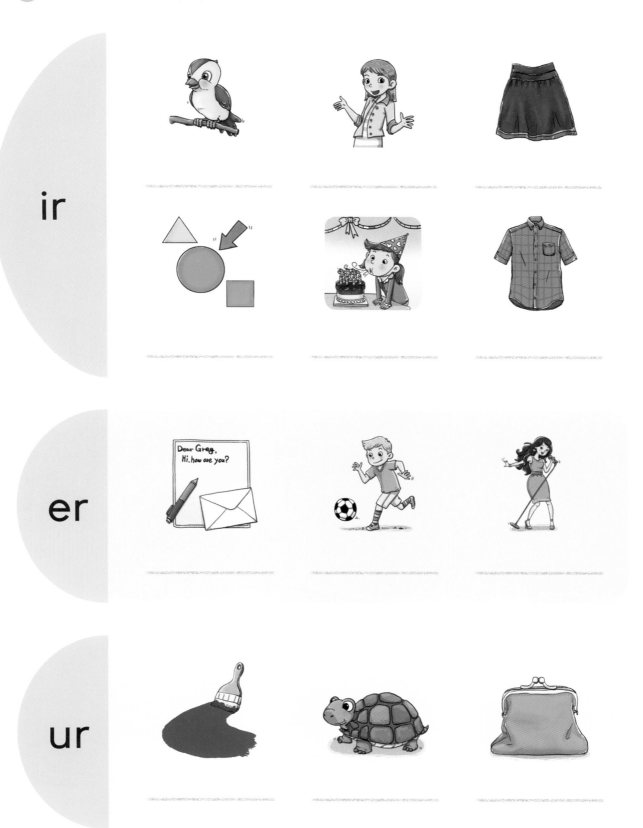

ir

er

ur

Match the letters and pictures.

1. **ou** •

• •

2. **ow** •

• •

3. **long oo** •

• •

4. **short oo** •

• •

5. **ar** •

• •

6. **ir** •

• •

Circle the word.

1.
corn
south
soccer

2.
owl
cow
turtle

3.
crown
food
wood

4.
look
hook
mouse

5.
farmer
fork
singer

6.
circle
park
root

7.
singer
purse
book

8.
letter
horn
store

9.
north
spoon
loud

Write the letters.

er   ou   oo(short)   ow   ur   ir   oo(long)   ar   or

1.

w [ ] [ ] d

2.

l [ ] [ ] d

3.

f [ ] [ ] k

4.

p [ ] [ ] se

5.

cl [ ] [ ] n

6.

m [ ] [ ] n

7.

sk [ ] [ ] t

8.

c [ ] [ ] d

9.

socc [ ] [ ]

Write the word.

1.

_____

2.

_____

3.

_____

4.

_____

5.

_____

6.

_____

7.

_____

8.

_____

9.

_____

10.

_____

11.

_____

12.

_____